GIVE ME LIBERTY!

Artist John Trumbull's impression of the Battle of Bunker Hill, June 17, 1775

Give Me Liberty!

The Story
of the Declaration
of Independence

RUSSELL FREEDMAN

HOLIDAY HOUSE / New York

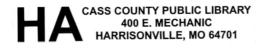

*For Brian
and Jessica*

www.holidayhouse.com

The text typeface is Caslon,
a design close in style to the original metal foundry type.
The ornament used on the title page, back of the jacket, and front case
is from Benjamin Franklin's title page for *A Collection of Charters and
Other Publick Acts Relating to the Province of Pennsylvania*, 1740.

Library of Congress Cataloging-in-Publication Data
Freedman, Russell.
Give me liberty!: the story of the Declaration of Independence / Russell Freedman.— 1st ed.
p. cm.
Includes bibliographical references (p.) and index.
Summary: Describes the events leading up to the Declaration of Independence as well
as the personalities and politics behind its framing.
ISBN 0-8234-1448-5 (hc.)
ISBN 0-8234-1753-0 (pbk.)
1. United States. Declaration of Independence—Juvenile literature. 2. United States—
Politics and government—1775–1783—Juvenile literature.
[1. United States. Declaration of Independence.
2. United States—Politics and government—1775–1783.] I. Title
E221 .F84 2000
973.3'13—dc21
99-057513
ISBN-13: 978-0-8234-1448-2 (hardcover)
ISBN-13: 978-0-8234-1753-7 (paperback)

Contents

The destruction of tea at Boston Harbor

1. The Night the Revolution Began:
The Boston Tea Party, December 16, 1773

William Gray, a master rope maker, knew there was going to be trouble in Boston that night. He wanted no part of it. As dusk fell, he closed the shutters of his house and shop. After supper, he sent his apprentice, fourteen-year-old Peter Slater, upstairs and locked the boy in his room.

Peter waited until the house was quiet. Then he knotted his bedding together, hung it out the window, and slid to freedom. He wasn't a rope maker's apprentice for nothing.

He hurried along dark cobbled streets to a secret meeting place, a blacksmith's shop where a crowd of men and boys seemed to be getting ready for a costume party. They were smearing their faces with coal dust and red paint and wrapping old blankets around their shoulders, disguising themselves as Mohawk Indians.

Carrying hatchets and clubs, the "Indians" emerged from hiding and marched to Griffin's Wharf, where three British merchant ships were tied up at the dock. The ships' holds were filled to bursting with 342 chests of fine blended tea, shipped from England by the East India Company and worth a king's ransom.

Dozens of other men and boys were arriving at Griffin's Wharf from all over Boston. Among them were blacksmiths, masons, shipwrights, shoemakers, farmers, laborers, merchants, and apprentices—even a few well-known citizens, men of prominent families and positions who had come along as lieutenants to direct the action and help keep order. These men had blackened and painted their faces with special care so they could not be recognized. They were running a great risk, for they planned to get rid of every pound of tea in the holds of those British ships. If their names became known, they could be arrested and tried for destroying the East India Company's property.

The Boston Tea Party was an act of defiance, a protest against the policies of the British Parliament and King George III, who ruled England's colonies in North America. The colonists objected to paying King George's taxes without having a voice in Parliament. They called it taxation without representation. And while the tax on tea was a small one, just three cents a pound, it was regarded as a symbol of British tyranny.

Throughout the thirteen colonies, people had boycotted British tea rather than pay the hated tax. The ports of New York and Philadelphia had refused to accept the East India Company's tea, and the ships had sailed back to London with their cargoes. At Charleston, South Carolina, the tea was unloaded, but then it was stored in damp warehouse vaults and left to rot.

In Boston, the three tea ships had been tied up at Griffin's Wharf for more than two weeks. When the ships refused to depart, a group of men calling themselves the Sons of Liberty hatched their secret plan to destroy the tea. All told, perhaps two hundred men and boys took part in the action. Divided into three groups, they boarded the ships, summoned the mates, demanded lanterns and keys, and went to work.

"Everything was as light as day, by the means of lamps and torches—a pin might be seen lying on the wharf," Robert Sessions recalled. The tea chests were hoisted up from the holds, broken open, and the tea dumped over the side into the moonlit waters of Boston Harbor.

"I never worked harder in my life," remembered Joshua Wyeth, who was fifteen at the time. "Although it was late in the evening when we began, we had discharged the whole three cargoes before the dawn of day."

Several thousand people had gathered to watch in silent approval from the wharf. Aboard the ships, great care was taken that the protest be carried out with discipline. Nothing but the tea was disturbed, and "not the least insult was offered to any person," John Andrews reported. After each hold had been emptied, the deck was

Dumping the tea overboard

swept clean. Everything left was put back in its proper place. Then a ship's officer was asked to come up on deck and see that no damage had been done—except to the tea, emptied from hundreds of chests, which was now floating away with the tide.

When all the tea had been thrown overboard, the "Mohawks" fell into line and marched away to the music of a fife, surprised that they had met no opposition. British warships anchored less than a quarter mile away had not attempted to interfere. In fact, the British admiral in charge of the fleet happened to be spending the night at a friend's house near Griffin's Wharf. He had watched the entire scene from an upstairs window.

As the marchers passed by, Admiral John Montague threw open the window, stuck out his head, and shouted, "Well, boys, you have had a fine, pleasant evening for your Indian caper—haven't you? But mind, you've got to pay the fiddler yet!"

"Oh, never mind!" one of the marchers shouted back. "Never mind, Squire! Just come out here if you please and we'll settle the bill in two minutes."

With that, Admiral Montague slammed the window shut.

Soon afterward, a rollicking new song was heard in the taverns of Boston and about the shops and wharves. It began like this:

Rally, Mohawks! Bring out your axes,
And tell King George we'll pay no taxes
    On his foreign tea. . . .

2. A New World

All that trouble over a three-cent tax on tea! The Boston Tea Party was the latest chapter in a family quarrel between England and her distant American colonies. England ruled her colonies like a stern parent who expects obedience. The colonists were acting like defiant offspring. "This is the Mother Country," declared the British statesman William Pitt. "They are the children. They must obey and we prescribe."

England insisted on its right to prescribe—to lay down the rules and laws that the colonists must obey. But the colonists were no longer willing to behave like dutiful children. They were demanding a greater voice in their own affairs.

A popular song written by Benjamin Franklin, called "The Mother Country," began like this:

We have an old Mother that peevish is grown,
She snubs us like Children that scarce walk alone;
She forgets we're grown up and have Sense of our own;
Which nobody can deny, deny, which nobody can deny.

If we don't obey Orders, whatever the Case;
She frowns, and she chides, and she loses all Pati-
Ence, and sometimes she hits us a Slap in the Face,
Which nobody can deny . . .

Charles Willson Peale's portrait
of Benjamin Franklin. The tenth son
of seventeen children of a soap and candle
maker, Franklin left school at the age of ten;
worked as an apprentice to his brother, a
printer; and became one of the most famous
and admired Americans of his time.

The first permanent English settlers had waded ashore at Jamestown and Plymouth in the early 1600s. They looked upon North America as a promising New World. While the continent may have been "new" and unknown to Europeans, to the peoples already living there, the Native Americans, it had been home for many thousands of years.

Over the next century and a half, thirteen English-speaking colonies were established along the Atlantic Coast from New Hampshire south to Georgia, with settlements stretching westward to the Appalachians. Beyond those mountains, the land was still Indian territory; the only colonists who ventured there were trappers, traders, and a few daring farmers who staked out homesteads in the forest wilderness.

By the 1770s, the colonies had more than 2.5 million inhabitants, including about five hundred thousand people of African descent, most of whom were enslaved. At first, the white settlers had come mainly from England, the Mother Country. But as word spread that the New World was a land of opportunity, immigrants began to arrive from all over western Europe. America was already becoming a melting pot of nationalities and religions.

At a tavern in Philadelphia, a visitor from Scotland found himself in "very mixed company. . . . There were Scots, English, Dutch, Germans, and Irish; there were Roman Catholicks, Church Men, Presbyterians, Quakers, Newlightmen, Methodists, Seventh day men, Moravians, Anabaptists, and one Jew. The whole company consisted of 25 [men] planted around an oblong table in a great hall and divided into committees in conversation. The prevailing topick was politicks."

The different religions were not always tolerant of one another. Quakers were not welcome in most of New England. Catholics were tolerated only in Maryland and Pennsylvania. And yet freedom of worship was a key feature of colonial life. Many immigrants had come to the New World to escape religious persecution.

Many others, lured by the promise of cheap land and the dream of prosperity, came in search of a better life. And often, their hopes were realized. Those who carved out a place for themselves in the wilderness or became skilled artisans in the flourishing towns were usually better off than they had been in their native countries.

Landing at Jamestown, 1607, from *Harper's Weekly,* June 2, 1860

Africans on a slave ship

When Benjamin Franklin visited Ireland in 1771, he was shocked by the poverty he saw. "They live in wretched hovels of mud and straw, are clothed in rags and subsist chiefly on potatoes," he told a friend. "Our New England farmers of the poorest sort are . . . princes when compared to them."

Immigrants who were too poor to pay for their passage across the Atlantic came over as indentured servants. They had to work their way to freedom. Indentured servants agreed to labor in America for a certain period, usually four to seven years, in exchange for their ship passage and their food, clothing, and lodging during their term of service. When their time was up, they were free to seek their fortunes. Since indentured servants lived under harsh conditions, many of them ran away. A captured servant who was not claimed by his master could be sold at public auction.

An indentured servant might be treated like a slave—but there was a big difference between the two. The servant had some legal rights and a limit to his term of service. The captured Africans who were shipped to America in chains and sold as slaves had no rights and no limit to their terms of service. Some slaves managed to escape or to buy their freedom. A few were freed by their masters. But most enslaved Africans and their children were slaves for life without hope of any future. They could be sold at any time, like horses or cattle.

By far the greatest number of enslaved Africans worked on farms and plantations in the South, but slavery existed to some degree in all the American colonies, and in fact throughout much of the world at that time. While American slavery was concentrated in the South, wealthy New England shipowners were the major carriers of slaves to the colonies. And while many colonial leaders spoke out against slavery, the profitable business of buying and selling humans was so common, it was taken for granted. In 1770, the Quakers became the first group in America to prohibit slave owning.

For white settlers, life in the colonies was a lot freer than it had been back home. America had its upper and lower classes, its rich and poor, but the class barriers that separated privileged aristocrats from lowly peasants in Europe seemed much less important in the New World. There were powerful landowners in the South and wealthy merchants in the towns of the North, but in America there was no titled nobility. The typical yeoman farmer owned rather than rented his land. A skilled artisan could become a prosperous and influential citizen. Shedding their European past, new immigrants in America were judged more by what they could do than by who their parents were.

Advertisement for a slave auction in Charleston, South Carolina

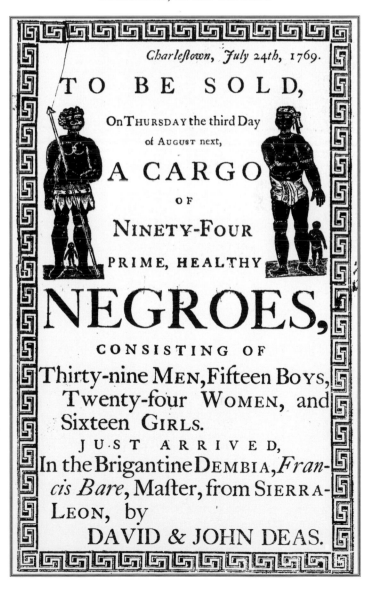

An unknown American artist painted this portrait of a well-to-do colonial family around 1790. The black servants standing in attendance behind the mother and children are probably slaves.

The colonists also enjoyed a high degree of self-government. As British subjects, they owed their allegiance to the king, who granted colonies charters and appointed colonial governors. England regulated the colonies' overseas trade and provided for their defense. Beyond that, the colonists ran their own affairs. They had their own legislatures, or assemblies, where their elected representatives passed laws and levied taxes.

As a rule, only men with property were allowed to vote, but "property" could mean almost any personal possessions that gave their owner a stake in the community. Except for slaves and indentured servants (who at times made up as much as half the colonial population), a substantial number of American men had a voice in local politics. In Boston during the 1770s, about 70 percent of adult males had voting rights—a larger base of support for government than could be found anywhere else in the world at that time.

At town meetings, according to one observer, "Each individual has an equal liberty of delivering his opinion, and is not liable to be silenced or browbeaten by a richer or greater townsman than himself; and each vote weighs equally whether that of the highest or lowest inhabitant."

Women were not allowed to vote. Although some had private tutors, girls did not even go to school. Colonial women supervised large plantations; ran farms, shops, and inns; engaged in many trades; raised huge families; and expressed their views freely. Eventually women fought in the Revolutionary War—but they did not vote. They would not win that right in America until 1920.

Visitors from Europe often commented on the independent spirit they found in the colonies. Americans were used to thinking for themselves. That is not surprising for a people who had braved a dangerous ocean voyage, blazed trails, cleared the land, built towns, and made most of their own laws. Having done all that, they meant to stand up for their rights.

A prosperous New England farm painted by artist and preacher Edward Hicks. A typical independent farmer owned 10 head of cattle, 16 sheep, 6 pigs, 2 horses, and a team of oxen.

3. "If This Be Treason"

Eight years before the Boston Tea Party, on May 29, 1765, a fiery back-woods lawyer with red hair and a golden tongue rose from his seat in the House of Burgesses in Williamsburg, Virginia. It was Patrick Henry's twenty-ninth birthday. He had been a member of the Virginia assembly for just ten days, but he made an electrifying speech that would be published and talked about throughout the colonies.

The British Parliament had just imposed an unpopular new tax on the Americans. It was called the Stamp Tax, and it provoked massive colonial opposition.

Patrick Henry addressing the Virginia assembly

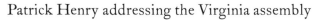

No one, said Patrick Henry, had a right to tax the people except their own elected representatives—men who would have to pay those taxes themselves. They were the only ones who could know which taxes the people could bear, and the best way to raise them.

When Henry denounced the Stamp Tax as a threat to liberty, some members of the assembly thought he was attacking King George personally. Shouts of "Treason! Treason!" came from all corners of the room.

"If this be treason," Henry reportedly cried out, "make the most of it!" Afterward, he was made to apologize and affirm his loyalty to the king.

The dispute over taxes and the authority of Parliament had been simmering ever since the French and

A powerful orator, Patrick Henry worked his way up from poverty to serve in the House of Burgesses, in the Continental Congress, and later as governor of Virginia.

Indian War, which had started in 1754. France and England, with their respective Indian allies, had fought for years to decide who would rule North America. The Iroquois of New York, a confederacy of six Indian nations, had sided with England. Most of the other Indians in the East had allied themselves with France.

The war ended in 1763 with a British victory. France was driven out of North America, but England was left with a gigantic war debt. The government had to raise money to pay that debt and to support the thousands of British troops who had been sent to patrol America's wilderness frontier.

King George and his ministers decided that the colonists should help pay some of these costs. And that is when the troubles started.

Americans had fought faithfully in the French and Indian War, battling side by side with British troops under British command. They had furnished money, too, piling up war debts of their own. In any case, they did not want all those British troops stationed in their midst. Every able-bodied man in the colonies between the ages of sixteen and sixty was in the militia and could be called up for active duty. The Americans felt perfectly capable of defending themselves.

More important, they insisted that they should not be taxed at all by the British Parliament, a legislature an ocean away in which they were not represented. It was their right as British subjects, they argued, to vote on their own taxes, in their own assemblies, as they had been doing all along.

At one time in the past, English kings and barons had exercised unlimited power to tax their people at will. They could take away a person's land and property without even giving a reason. If that person protested, he could be thrown into a dungeon and left to die.

A skirmish in the French and Indian War

Over centuries of sometimes bloody struggle, the English people won a succession of rights that curbed the power of their kings and laid the foundations of representative government. Along with such rights as free speech and trial by jury, they won the right to decide for themselves, through their elected representatives, how much they should be taxed. Without that right, people would be at the mercy of a tyrant, who could tax them endlessly and unfairly. He could keep them poor and subservient forever.

The Americans objected to Parliament taking money out of their pockets without their consent. And they had other complaints as well. Parliament had passed strict laws governing the colonies' overseas trade, laws that the Americans felt were unfair. Another law called the Quartering Act ordered the colonists to provide barracks, food, and other supplies for the British troops stationed among them, and that caused more resentment.

Could Parliament impose any laws it wanted on the American colonies, even though the Americans had no voice in Parliament? Or was there a limit to Parliament's authority?

The Stamp Act, passed in 1765, finally brought matters to a head. The colonists would now have to buy British tax stamps to paste on all printed material issued in America—a stamp for each page of a newspaper or pamphlet; for every will, contract, marriage license, and diploma—even for playing cards, calendars, and advertisements.

The colonists were outraged. "Taxation without representation is tyranny!" became an angry cry heard everywhere.

That summer a storm of protest swept through the colonies. Demonstrators organized by the Sons of Liberty threatened to seize and destroy the hated tax stamps and force the royal tax commissioners to give up their posts. In Boston, a rioting mob demolished the building where tax commissioner Andrew Oliver had planned to distribute his

The Stamp Act riots in Boston

This American cartoon expresses the colonists' opposition to the Stamp Act.

stamps. Then the crowd marched to Oliver's nearby mansion. "They pulled down the Garden Fence of Mr. Oliver," a bystander reported, "entered his House, drank some of his Wine, and broke some Windows. They would not have entered his House had it not been for some irritating Language from those within."

The next day, Oliver resigned.

In New York, Major Thomas James, commander of the British garrison, boasted that he would cram the tax stamps down American throats at the point of his sword. That evening, some two thousand tax protesters stormed the major's elegant house and tore the place apart.

Women did not take to the streets, but they made their views known by banding together in societies called the Daughters of Liberty. The colonists had pledged to boycott English goods. They would refuse to buy anything made in England, especially cloth, a mainstay of the British economy. The Daughters of Liberty gathered in churches, courthouses, and meeting halls to spin and weave their own cloth. In place of fine British wools and brocades, sturdy homespun cloth became the patriotic fashion.

Paul Revere, a burly Boston silversmith and active member of the Sons of Liberty, summed up the dispute in a letter to a cousin: "If they have the right to take one shilling from us without our consent, they have the right to all we possess, for it is the birthright of an Englishman, not to be taxed without the consent of himself, or Representative."

On the day the Stamp Act was to take effect, not a single tax commissioner was in business anywhere in America. When it became obvious that the tax could never be collected, Parliament backed down. The Stamp Act was repealed. But King George and his ministers were determined to show that England had the right to levy taxes anywhere in the empire. In 1767, they pressured Parliament to pass the Townshend Acts, which levied taxes on British imports in America such as paper, glass, lead, paints, and tea, the most popular beverage in the colonies.

This British cartoon satirizes the American women who joined together as the Daughters of Liberty.

Again, the Americans resisted. They organized a new boycott of British goods that was so effective, imports from England were cut in half. Now it was the turn of the English merchants to protest. The boycott was costing them a fortune.

Parliament again gave in and in 1770 repealed all the Townshend taxes except for one—a three-penny-per-pound tax on tea. It was a small tax, disguised as an import duty, but it was kept on the books to demonstrate that Parliament still had the right to levy taxes on Americans.

Meanwhile, Britain had stationed troops in several colonial towns to help keep order—and that led to more trouble. Two infantry regiments and an artillery company were sent to Boston. Resentful citizens watched sullenly as the soldiers in their scarlet coats marched up King Street, with drums beating and fifes playing, and pitched their tents on Boston Common.

Soon, insults and scuffles broke out between citizens and soldiers. Boys ran after the redcoats, hooting "Bloody-backs!" and "Lobsters for sale!" Soldiers were "accidentally" jostled off bridges and wharves. And on the evening of March 5, 1770, this mounting tension exploded in the snow-covered streets of Boston.

Paul Revere's engraving of the Boston Massacre shows
British soldiers mowing down helpless citizens.

This painting by Alonzo Chappel is a more accurate portrayal of what actually happened at the Boston Massacre. It shows the redcoats firing in self-defense as a mob threatens to attack them.

An unruly crowd of about four hundred men had collected in front of the Customs House, where eight British soldiers were standing guard. The men jeered and shouted insults. They threw rocks, oyster shells, and chunks of ice; threatened the soldiers with clubs; and pressed up close to the muzzles of their guns, daring them to fire.

Then someone—it was never clear who—actually did shout "Fire!" The frightened soldiers leveled their muskets and pulled the triggers. When

Crispus Attucks, a six-foot-two-inch former slave, was one of five men killed in the Boston Massacre.

the smoke cleared, five Bostonians lay dead or dying on the frozen ground. One of the victims was Crispus Attucks, a towering sailor and former slave of black and American Indian ancestry. Later, he was said to be the first black man to die in the Revolutionary War. Perhaps 10,000 people marched in the funeral procession for the five dead men, out of a total Boston population of 16,000.

To avoid further trouble, the British pulled their troops out of Boston and stationed them at a nearby harbor fort. The eight soldiers who had fired their muskets were arrested and tried for murder in a Boston court. They were defended by John Adams, a scrappy little Massachusetts lawyer and a leading member of the Sons of Liberty.

Adams hated the presence of British troops in Boston as much as anyone. But he believed that the soldiers had a right to protect themselves and were entitled to a fair trial, so he agreed to take their case—an act of courage, since so many Bostonians were demanding that the soldiers be punished. During the trial, rocks were thrown through Adams's windows, and boys jeered him on the street.

Adams argued in court that the soldiers had defended themselves against a lawless mob. When the jury delivered its verdict, six of the defendants were acquitted. The other two were convicted of manslaughter, a lesser offense than murder. They were branded on their thumbs and released.

But that was not the end of it. John Adams had an older cousin named Samuel Adams, a shrewd political activist who had led the opposition to the Stamp Act. Samuel Adams knew how to sway public opinion. He called the Customs House shootings "the Boston Massacre," and he had his good friend Paul Revere make a copper engraving that showed

British soldiers mowing down peaceful Bostonians. Revere's portrayal of the shooting was not accurate, but it was printed by the thousands and circulated all over the colonies—a powerful piece of propaganda that would help pave the way toward a revolution.

John Singleton Copley's portrait of John Adams, the Massachusetts lawyer who defended the British soldiers at their trial following the Boston Massacre. He later became the first vice president and second president of the United States.

Samuel Adams was a founder of the Sons of Liberty. He also came up with the idea for the Committees of Correspondence, which were organized in towns throughout the colonies. In an era when letters were the only means of long-distance communication, these committees began to write back and forth. They became a network for exchanging information and planning common action to resist British policies.

After the Boston Massacre, things quieted down for a while. The Americans continued to boycott British tea, drinking "liberty tea" made from local herbs or smuggled-in Dutch tea. The British tried to break the boycott by shipping large amounts of low-cost tea to America, but the tea still carried that despised tax.

On November 28, 1773, the British tea ship *Dartmouth* docked at Griffin's Wharf in Boston. The next morning, the town was plastered with broadsides:

> Friends! Brethren! Countrymen! That worst of Plagues, the detested tea shipped for this port by the East India Company, is now arrived in the Harbour; the hour of destruction or manly opposition to . . . Tyranny, stares you in the Face.

Two more ships, the *Beaver* and the *Eleanor*, soon joined the *Dartmouth* at Griffin's Wharf. On board they had 342 chests of tea, valued at 18,000 British pounds.

By early December, thousands of protesters were attending mass meetings that filled Boston's Old South Church and overflowed to the streets outside. Speaker after speaker condemned the tea tax, demanding that the ships leave Boston and return to London with their cargoes. But Governor Thomas Hutchinson of Massachusetts refused to allow the ships to depart. He insisted that the tea be unloaded.

It was then that the militant Sons of Liberty, meeting secretly at the

Green Dragon Tavern, began to hatch their plan to board the British ships and throw the offending tea overboard. Finally, on the evening of December 16, Samuel Adams stood up at a mass meeting and shouted to the crowd: "This meeting can do nothing more to save the country!"

From the balcony of Old South Church, from its dark galleries and corridors, came war whoops and yells: "To Griffin's Wharf!" and "Boston Harbor a teapot tonight!"

Men were shouting, running about, racing out of the building as John Hancock, another leading Son of Liberty, cried out above the commotion: "Let every man do what is right in his own eyes!"

That was a signal for the Boston Tea Party to begin. All over Boston, men and boys disguised themselves as Mohawk Indians and headed for the British tea ships at Griffin's Wharf.

4. Intolerable Acts

When news of the Boston Tea Party finally reached England, King George was furious. He demanded that the colonists be punished for their "violent and outrageous" behavior. They must be taught a lesson!

King George III of England wearing his coronation robes

Prodded by the king and his ministers, Parliament passed a series of harsh laws designed to make an example of Massachusetts. The colony was placed under strict military rule. Town meetings, by which the colonists governed themselves, were curtailed. Local officials would be appointed by the military governor rather than be elected. Americans accused of certain crimes could be shipped off to England for trial, bypassing local juries. And under the strict new Quartering Act, British troops occupying the colony could be housed in private homes as well as in unoccupied buildings, whether the home owners liked it or not.

To make matters worse, Boston Harbor was to be closed to all shipping until the colonists paid in full for the ruined tea. Since the town was a major sea-port, its economy would be crippled. Bostonians would not even be able to fish in their own waters.

These punishing laws were intended to bring the rebellious colonists to their knees. "We must control them or submit to them," thundered Frederick, Lord North, the king's prime minister.

The colonists called the offensive new laws the Intolerable Acts. Even before the laws took effect, express riders galloped out of Boston with urgent letters in their saddlebags, calling on the other colonies for aid. In Virginia, the House of Burgesses denounced the British occupation as a "military invasion" and declared that an attack on one colony was an attack on all. If the people of Massachusetts could be bullied and deprived of their rights, then no colony was safe.

Delegates leaving Carpenters' Hall in Philadelphia after a session of the First Continental Congress

The Virginians called for a meeting of all the colonies to decide what to do next. Word was spread from town to town through the Committees of Correspondence, and that summer every colony except Georgia named delegates to attend a Continental Congress in Philadelphia, America's leading city with a population of 40,000.

Fifty-five delegates met in Philadelphia's brand-new Carpenters' Hall on September 5, 1774. They had traveled to the Congress on horse-back, in carriages, and in stagecoaches, eating and sleeping at inns along the way. Most of them had never met before. Among them were plantation owners, merchants, lawyers, teachers, ministers, farmers, and physicians. On the whole, they were men of wealth and social position, leaders in their communities who held university degrees, knew Latin and Greek, and wore lace ruffles at their wrists and silver buckles on their shoes. They hardly seemed like a gathering of rebels.

The delegates had come together with a common goal—to agree, if possible, on measures they might take to defend their rights. "All America is thrown into one mass," delegate Patrick Henry declared. "The distinctions between Virginians, Pennsylvanians, New Yorkers, and New Englanders are no more. I am not a Virginian, but an American!"

The delegates soon found themselves divided into opposing camps. The moderates and conservatives argued that Americans must find a way to get along with England. They should rely on the unwritten British constitution, which granted them the same rights and privileges guaranteed to all British subjects. The radicals disagreed. They wanted a greater voice in their own affairs. They believed that their liberties were being threatened, and that they might have to resort to arms.

At that time, hardly anyone was willing to speak openly of American independence. Yet no one favored obedience to Britain at any price. Nearly all the delegates hoped for a peaceful solution to the crisis that would allow the colonies to remain within the British empire.

George Washington, a delegate from Virginia, was regarded as a moderate. He opposed Britain's policies, but he was so reserved in his manner that he remained quietly in the background and said little. Even so, the other delegates kept an eye on him, mindful of his reputation as a hero in the French and Indian War. They were impressed by his dignified military bearing and surprised by how young the six-foot-two-inch, forty-two-year-old ex-colonel looked. "He is a soldier, a warrior," said one delegate, yet "a modest man; sensible; speaks little—in action cool, like a bishop at his prayers."

John Adams and Samuel Adams, delegates from Massachusetts,

sided with the radicals. They agreed with Patrick Henry that the colonies should form a government and go to war, if necessary, to defend their liberties. But for the time being, they kept these opinions to themselves. John Adams noted that a great many delegates shrank from any mention of "independency" and "shuddered at the prospect of blood."

John Adams—short, stout, temperamental, and talkative—was a respected political thinker and writer. He would soon quit his law practice and devote himself to the colonies' struggle for independence. His cousin Samuel was a tireless man of action, a firebrand who was constantly organizing committees and leading demonstrations. Politics were his passion.

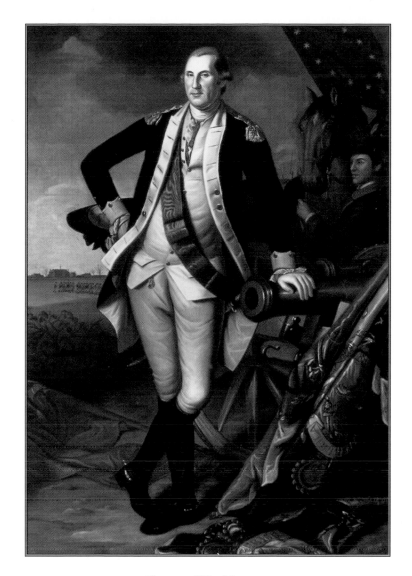

George Washington

Some delegates admired Samuel Adams as a political idealist, a visionary. Others saw him as a crank, a revolutionary fanatic, a rabble-rouser who "eats little, drinks little, sleeps little, thinks much, and is most decisive . . . in the pursuit of his objectives." A rumpled man with a kindly face, magnetic blue eyes, and an iron will, he cared nothing about wealth, social position, or appearance. His clothes were so shabby that friends in Boston bought him a new outfit so that he would not

John Singleton Copley's portrait
of Samuel Adams. Adams was
a founder
of the Sons of Liberty and
the chief organizer of
the Boston Tea Party.

embarrass Massachusetts when he went to Congress. Those who knew him were astounded when he showed up in Philadelphia wearing a handsome wine red suit and carrying a gold-handled cane.

The delegates met for seven weeks, debating their differences and trying to agree on a course of action. Before adjourning, they pledged their support to beleagured Massachusetts. They set up the Continental Association to shut off trade with England. And they passed several resolutions condemning British interference in colonial affairs and demanding that Parliament repeal all those laws that infringed on their liberties.

But they also sent a respectful petition to King George and the British people. "Permit us to be as free as yourselves," they said, "and we shall ever esteem a union with you to be our greatest glory and our greatest happiness."

Even as they spoke of peace, the delegates warned their fellow citizens that war might come. Throughout the colonies, able-bodied men were forming active militia companies and drilling with guns on village greens. Along with the regular militia, special fifty-man units, whose members were called minutemen, were ready to rush into action at a moment's notice.

People everywhere were beginning to take sides. Those who supported the king, who wanted to remain British subjects, were known as Loyalists, or Tories. Colonists who leaned toward independence called themselves Patriots, or Whigs. Bitter arguments broke out as members of the same family found themselves in opposing camps. And as the

Minutemen leaving their farms and families to take up arms against the British

colonies edged closer to revolution, deeply felt political differences would shatter friendships and tear some families apart.

In Virginia, the royal governor had dissolved the House of Burgesses and forbidden its members to hold meetings in Williamsburg, the capital. Instead, they met defiantly at St. John's Church in Richmond. It was there that Patrick Henry took the floor on March 23, 1775, to deliver a rousing call to arms.

Henry reminded his fellow assemblymen that Massachusetts was still under military occupation. The Massachusetts assembly, like the House of Burgesses, had been dissolved. The liberty of the colonies was threatened. "Gentlemen may cry peace, peace, but there is no peace," he declared. "The war is actually begun!"

Patrick Henry cried out:
"Give me liberty, or give me death!"

As Henry spoke, he stood in the church aisle with his head bowed, his arms held out stiffly before him, his wrists crossed as if manacled. "An unearthly fire burned in his eye," according to one account. "His voice rose louder and louder, until the walls of the building, and all within them, seemed to shake and rock."

Henry cried out: "Is life so dear, or peace so sweet, as to be purchased at the price of chains and slavery? Forbid it, Almighty God! I know not what course others may take, but as for me, *give me liberty, or give me death*!"

With those words, Henry flung open his arms as if casting off his chains. Then he slammed his fist against his chest as if driving a dagger into his heart.

Events were now being swept along by a whirlwind of political passions. In England, King George refused to consider the petition sent by the Continental Congress. To do so, said the king, would make it seem that "the Mother Country" was "afraid" of her rebellious children. The king's ministers rejected any talk of a negotiated settlement. They persuaded Parliament to declare the colony of Massachusetts in a state of rebellion.

Orders were sent to General Thomas Gage, the British military governor in Boston, telling him it was time to act. He was to break up the revolutionary com-

John Singleton Copley's portrait of John Hancock, a leading member of the Sons of Liberty and the wealthiest merchant in Boston. He later became governor of Massachusetts.

mittees that had been recruiting militiamen, arrest the rebel "ringleaders," and ship them off to London in chains to be tried for high treason.

General Gage identified two men—Samuel Adams and John Hancock—as leaders of the rebellion. Hancock was the wealthiest merchant in Boston, a prominent member of the Sons of Liberty, and an organizer, with

Samuel Adams, of the Boston Tea Party. People said, "Sam Adams writes the letters and John Hancock pays the postage." Both men had just been named delegates to the Second Continental Congress, scheduled to meet in Philadelphia in May 1775. They had been elected by the outlawed Massachusetts assembly, which had been meeting secretly in the town of Concord.

Before General Gage could arrest Hancock and Adams, the two men went into hiding at the home of Hancock's sister in Lexington, a farming town about fifteen miles from Boston. While Gage was trying to track them down, his spies informed him that the rebels had stockpiled a hundred barrels of gunpowder and fourteen cannons at Concord, about five miles beyond Lexington. Gage decided on a show of force. A surprise march on Concord to seize the munitions would have a crippling effect on the rebel forces.

The British general was confident that he could accomplish this seizure without firing a shot. The rebels had been described in Parliament as "raw, undisciplined, cowardly men," amateur soldiers who "would never dare to face a British army."

5. The Shot Heard 'Round the World: *April 19, 1775*

General Gage had his spies, and the rebels had theirs. The rebels had been tipped off that the British were planning a secret night march to seize the munitions at Concord and to arrest Samuel Adams and John Hancock. But they hadn't learned which way the redcoats would march.

Boston sat on a peninsula linked to the mainland by a narrow strip of land called Boston Neck. The British soldiers could leave town by land, marching across Boston Neck, or they could go by water, crossing Back Bay in longboats.

Two adventurous Sons of Liberty volunteered to ride into the countryside and spread the alarm that the British were coming. The riders would take off in different directions so that if one man was captured, the other might still get through. William Dawes, a Boston tanner, was to sneak past the British sentries at Boston Neck, hightail it to Lexington, where Adams and Hancock were hiding, then ride on to Concord.

The other night rider was Boston silversmith Paul Revere. He was to cross the Charles River in a rowboat and mount a waiting horse on the opposite shore.

Before leaving, Revere arranged for friends to place two signal lanterns in the bell tower of Old North Church, the tallest structure in

John Singleton Copley's
portrait of
Boston silversmith
Paul Revere

Boston. They would light one lantern if the British troops left Boston by land, two lanterns if they went by sea.

Revere was well on his way before the lanterns flashed their signal. Accompanied by his dog, he left his house and joined two fellow Patriots who had agreed to row him across the river. As they climbed into the boat, the story goes, Revere realized he had forgotten his spurs, so he sent the dog trotting home with a note tied to its collar. When the dog returned, the note was gone and a pair of spurs was in its place.

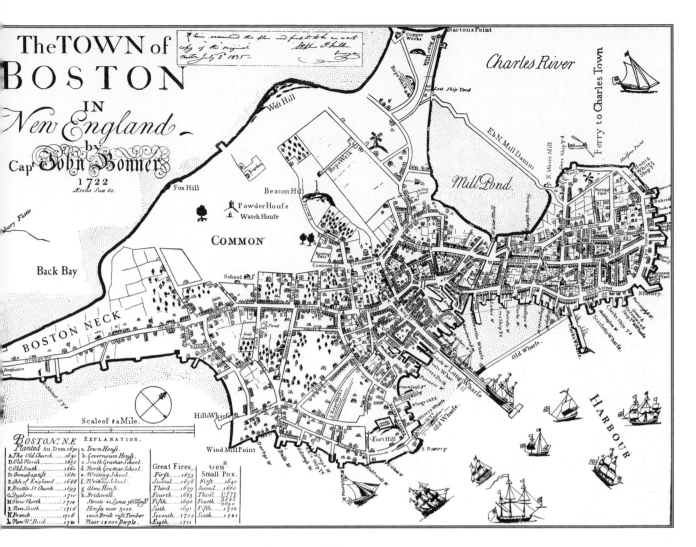

The TOWN of BOSTON IN New England by Capt. John Bonner 1722

Charles River

Ferry to Charles Town

Mill Pond

COMMON

Back Bay

BOSTON NECK

HARBOUR

Fox Hill

Beacon Hill
Powder Houfe
Watch Houfe

School

Wind Mill Point

Fort Hill

Scale of ¼ a Mile.

An early map of Boston

Rowing quietly, Revere and his comrades set out across the river. They stayed well downstream from the looming hulk of the sixty-four-gun British warship *Somerset*, whose great hempen anchor cable was creaking and groaning like a ghost in the night. On the far shore, other Patriots waited with a swift mare named Brown Beauty. By the time Revere joined them, they had seen two signal lanterns glimmer in the distant church steeple. The British troops were already on their way across Back Bay.

Paul Revere's midnight ride: "I alarumed almost every house."

It was 11:00 P.M. when Revere set off on his famous midnight ride, galloping hard through the night. "The moon shone bright," he remembered. "I alarumed almost every house—shouting 'The regulars are out!'—till I got to Lexington."

He reached Lexington at about the same time as William Dawes. They went straight to the house where Adams and Hancock were staying and warned them to make their escape. Hancock called for his musket and sword. He declared himself ready to join the minutemen who were assembling on Lexington Common. Adams talked him out of it. "That is not our business," he said. He convinced Hancock that he would be of no use if he were captured or killed, and the two men prepared to slip away before the redcoats arrived.

Revere and Dawes, meanwhile, set out for Concord. On the way they met another Patriot, Dr. Samuel Prescott, who had been visiting his fiancée in Lexington that night. Prescott joined them.

The three men had not gone far before a British patrol spotted them and shouted for them to halt. Prescott and Dawes got away, jumping their horses over a stone wall. Revere was cut off as he rode for a nearby clump of woods. "They threatened to blow my brains out," he recalled. He managed to talk his way out of trouble, but that was the end of his midnight ride. The redcoats took Brown Beauty, and Revere had to trudge back to Lexington on foot, hobbled by his silver spurs and heavy riding boots.

In Lexington, the meetinghouse bell was tolling the alarm. Minutemen were rushing out of their houses, galloping in from nearby

Paul Revere's capture by a British patrol:
"They threatened to blow my brains out."

farms, and mustering on the village green. Most of them were family men in their thirties or forties. There were a dozen teenagers, eight fathers with sons at their sides, and some grandfathers. They were armed with muskets, squirrel guns, and fowling pieces. Some of the men had bayonets, while many carried hatchets, a weapon they had discovered while fighting the Indians. There was at least one black face among them, an African slave named Prince Estabrook who had volunteered to fight. He was admitted to the company by a majority vote.

Captain John Parker, the leader of the militia, is said to have told his men: "Stand your ground. Don't fire unless fired upon. But if they mean to have a war, let it begin here!"

The sun was rising as the British troops came into view, marching up the road in quick time. There were about 200 redcoats in the advance column, with perhaps another 600 bringing up the rear. Waiting for them were no more than 60 or 70 minutemen.

An officer at the head of the British column, Major John Pitcairn, rode up on his horse. He gestured with his sword and called out, "Lay down your arms, you damned rebels, and disperse!"

The minutemen hesitated. At an order from Captain Parker, they began to move away slowly, as if to let the redcoats pass. Then someone fired a gun. Each side would claim later that the other side fired that first shot.

The British troops lowered their muskets and discharged a full volley directly into the minutemen's ranks. The Americans began to shoot back as the redcoats charged forward, lunging with their bayonets. The fighting lasted only minutes before the British commander, Colonel Francis Smith, rode into the center of the chaotic scene, waving his sword and shouting, "Cease fire! Cease fire!"

When the smoke cleared, eight Americans lay dead or dying, with ten more clutching bleeding wounds. Women and children ran screaming

The battle on Lexington Green

from nearby houses and rushed to their loved ones. One British officer had been wounded in the leg.

As the stunned townspeople looked on, the redcoats re-formed their ranks and fired a victory volley into the air, followed by three cheers. Then, with drums beating and fifes playing, they marched off to Concord, five miles away.

Warned that the British were coming, the people of Concord had spent the night hiding arms and gunpowder in covered pits dug in the woods. By the time the British columns arrived at about 8:00 A.M., three companies of minutemen had stationed themselves on a hill overlooking the village. They knew that shots had been fired at Lexington, but they hadn't yet learned that eight of their countrymen had been killed there.

The Americans were still outnumbered, but their ranks were growing rapidly as reinforcements rode in from the countryside. They did not want bloodshed, and they knew that the munitions were safely hidden, so they stood by watchfully as the British soldiers marched into Concord and began a house-to-house search for arms.

After a while, the redcoats found some wooden gun carriages, piled them in the street, and started a bonfire. When the minutemen on the hill saw smoke rising from the village, they thought that the British had set fire to some houses. "Are you going to let them burn the town down?" one man shouted.

With that, the minutemen marched down the hill and started to cross the North Bridge over the Concord River into Concord. The British

Minutemen rushing off to join the battle at Concord

detachment guarding the bridge tried to stop them, but the Americans ignored the warning shots and kept coming.

Finally, the redcoats fired a volley at the head of the American column. Two minutemen fell dead—one man shot through the heart, the other through the head. The Americans fired back, aiming at the scarlet coats massed on the other side of the bridge, instantly killing three British soldiers. As the minutemen stormed across the bridge, the redcoats panicked and ran for their lives. They stampeded back down the road into Concord, trailed by wounded men "hobbling and a'running and looking back to see if we was after them."

The poet Ralph Waldo Emerson would later write the lines now inscribed on a monument at the site of Concord's North Bridge:

By the rude bridge that arched the flood,
Their flag to April's breeze unfurled,
Here once the embattled farmers stood,
And fired the shot heard round the world.

The British had expected to encounter a bunch of simple farmers— "raw, undisciplined, cowardly men" who would break and run at the first volley. But these "embattled farmers" had proven themselves crack shots, ready to defend their families and communities. And more of them were galloping in from the surrounding area all the time. Colonel Smith, the British commander, gave up any plans for a counterattack. He worried about getting himself and his men back to Boston alive.

By then, everyone had heard about the battle at Lexington, and the Americans were bent on revenge. As the British troops began their withdrawal from Concord, swarms of minutemen followed, dodging and twisting through the fields and woods, fighting Indian style as they sniped at the redcoats from all sides, firing from house windows, from

The fight at Concord's North Bridge

behind stone walls and barns, ambushing the retreating soldiers at every turn in the country road. Soon "a grait many Lay dead and the Road was bloddy," a British corporal wrote.

The British march back to Boston disintegrated into a panicky rout. "We began to run rather than retreat in order," said one officer.

The hounded redcoats were saved from disaster by a relief party of a thousand fresh troops sent out from Boston. But the wild retreat continued all that afternoon. One of the bloodiest battles was fought in the crossroads village of Menotomy (present-day Arlington), where 40 Americans and 40 British soldiers died in savage house-to-house, hand-to-hand fighting.

It was nearly dark when the battered British troops, carrying their wounded, straggled to safety in Charlestown, across the river from Boston. During the last skirmish that day, British soldiers saw a black man hit by a bullet and dragged to safety by the minutemen fighting beside him. It may have been Prince Estabrook, the slave who had volunteered to fight with the Lexington militia. Estabrook recovered from his wound, served in the American army for the rest of the war, and won his freedom through his military service. Other black militiamen who stood against the British that day included Pompy of Braintree, Prince of Brookline, Cato Wood of Menotomy, and Peter Salem of Framingham.

Some 3,700 Americans from 23 townships had joined in the fighting, battling 1,800 British regulars. The British side lost 272 men killed, wounded, or missing. The Americans counted 94 casualties in all, although many of their wounded may simply have limped home and never reported their injuries.

Sir Hugh Percy, commander of the brigade that went to the relief of the British expedition, was astounded by the persistence of the Americans and impressed by the tactical skill of their commanders. "Whoever dares to look at them as an irregular mob, will find himself much mistaken," he said. "They have men amongst them who know very well what they are about."

Chasing the redcoats back to Boston

6. "The Whites of Their Eyes": *June 17, 1775*

After the redcoats were chased back to Boston, express riders galloped into the countryside, carrying news of the fighting at Lexington and Concord. "The whole country became as if it were electrified," remembered John Adlum, a sixteen-year-old volunteer militiaman, "and almost everyone, young and old, were formed into companies."

All across New England, armed companies of Patriots set out to join the militia camped outside Boston. Soon there were more than ten thousand of these volunteers. They began to build guard posts and fortifications that would blockade all roads leading out of Boston and imprison the British garrison inside the town.

General Gage, the British military governor, had agreed to let citizens leave Boston before the blockade began, provided the rebels gave safe conduct to any Loyalists who might want to join the British troops. For several days the roads were jammed with refugees carrying bundles and leading strings of children as Patriot families streamed out of town and Loyalists streamed in.

Throughout the colonies, every local militia company was on the alert, ready for a possible showdown with Britain. And in the midst of these warlike preparations, on May 10, 1775, the Second Continental

Setting out to join the militia

Congress met in Philadelphia—this time at the Pennsylvania State House, known today as Independence Hall.

A number of prominent men from the First Continental Congress returned, including John Hancock, who was elected president of this new congress; John and Samuel Adams; and George Washington. Colonel Washington arrived on horseback wearing his old buff-and-blue militia uniform—a sign that he was ready, if necessary, to fight.

Among the new delegates were thirty-two-year-old Thomas Jefferson from Virginia, a studious lawyer and plantation owner who was known to be a good writer; and sixty-nine-year-old Benjamin Franklin, probably the best-known American of the time. Franklin had just returned from England, where he had spent several years as the American agent for several colonies. He sat as a member of the Pennsylvania delegation, attended every session, was both witty and grave, and never hesitated to express his radical views. Franklin was for independence.

Many of his fellow delegates disagreed. Despite the fighting at Lexington and Concord, they were not yet willing to break away from England. They still hoped for a peaceful settlement of the colonies' dispute with the Mother Country.

As the delegates were meeting and debating, word reached Philadelphia

Thomas Jefferson as a young man

that a small force of American volunteers, led by Ethan Allen and Benedict Arnold, had captured British-held Fort Ticonderoga on Lake Champlain in northern New York. On the morning of May 10—the day the Congress had convened—the Americans had seized the wilderness fort in a surprise raid at dawn, without losing a man. The fort was critical because it guarded the northern approaches to the Hudson River and the city of New York. Now it belonged to the Americans, along with all its cannons, mortars, howitzers, and cannonballs. Benedict Arnold would later go over to the British side and be branded a traitor, but in May 1775, he was still a dedicated Patriot.

After meeting for more than a month, the Continental Congress reached an important decision. Massachusetts had asked the Congress to take charge of the growing force of militiamen outside Boston. On June 14, the delegates voted to adopt the New England troops as part of an "American Continental Army," and to appropriate funds for the army's support.

Once Congress had established an official army, the delegates had to appoint a commanding general. The militiamen already had a general they trusted, Artemas Ward of Massachusetts. But Ward, like his men, was a New Englander, and the delegates felt that a truly national army had to represent all the colonies.

John Adams rose to nominate a Southerner—Virginia's George Washington. Adams hailed Washington as America's foremost soldier, a man whose "skill and experience as an officer, whose independent fortune, great talents and excellent universal character" would unite the colonies "better than any other person in the Union."

Washington was sitting near the door. "As he heard me allude to him," Adams recalled, "from his usual modesty [he] darted into the library rooms," where he waited quietly while the delegates debated his nomination.

Washington was elected unanimously. He was grateful for the honor, he said, but he recognized the difficulties he would face. Great Britain was the most powerful nation on earth. Her troops had won laurels in every quarter of the globe. The Americans, Washington wrote later, were "not then organized as a nation, or known as a people upon the earth. We had no preparation. Money, the nerve of war, was wanting."

Washington would be in command of a ragtag army of volunteers who had little training and scarcely enough gunpowder to keep their weapons firing. "I beg it may be remembered," he told his fellow dele-

Ethan Allen and Benedict Arnold capture Fort Ticonderoga
in a surprise raid at dawn.

John Adams proposes George Washington as commander
of the Continental Army.

gates, "that I, this day, declare with the utmost sincerity I do not think
myself equal to the command." He would accept no salary, he insisted,
but would serve without pay for a cause he believed to be just.

Before Washington could travel to Boston to take up his command, a
new battle erupted. British warships had sailed into Boston Harbor, carrying reinforcements for the troops who were bottled up inside the town.
When the rebels learned that the British were planning a massive attack,
they acted quickly to defend themselves.

North of Boston, across the Charles River, two hills—Breed's Hill and
Bunker Hill—looked out over the town and commanded a wide area all
around. On the night of June 16, under cover of darkness, 1,200 New
England militiamen occupied both hills and began to build fortifications
on Breed's Hill, which was lower than Bunker Hill but closer to Boston. As
the British slept, the rebels worked furiously, digging trenches and erecting
thick earthen walls. At daybreak, a British officer on a warship in the harbor

peered through his spyglass and saw that an American fort had gone up overnight, putting British ships within range of American artillery.

British guns opened up, firing from warships, from floating batteries, and from Copp's Hill in Boston. The British cannons could not be elevated high enough to hit their mark directly, but a few cannonballs scudded up the hill and crashed into the fort. One of them tore off a militiaman's head—the battle's first casualty. Before his comrades could panic, Colonel William Prescott leaped up on the earthen parapet and stood there defiantly, showing his men that there wasn't much danger of anyone else being hit.

The Battle of Bunker Hill

Watching the bombardment of Charlestown
from Boston's rooftops

At about three that afternoon, two thousand British troops crossed the Charles River in barges and prepared to storm the rebel fort. They began their orderly advance at the foot of Breed's Hill, trudging up the steep slope through high summer grass under a blistering sun. The temperature had soared into the nineties. Each redcoat was carrying a full pack that included three days' rations and weighed 125 pounds. The British expected to chase the rebels off the hill and pursue them all the way into Cambridge, where the Americans had their headquarters and supplies.

The rebels, meanwhile, had received several hundred reinforcements. They were armed with every imaginable kind of rifle and musket. The lead pipes from the organ of Christ's Church in Cambridge had been melted down to make bullets, but still there weren't enough bullets to go around. Some of the rebels loaded their muskets with sharp pieces of iron and old nails.

The Americans waited at the top of Breed's Hill behind their earthen walls. Their officers moved among them, urging them to stay calm, ordering them to save their fire until the last possible moment. "Don't fire until you see the whites of their eyes," the men were told.

When the advancing redcoats were about forty yards from the fort, the rebels let loose with a deadly barrage of gunfire that ripped into the British columns, throwing the redcoats back, leaving the hillside littered with bodies and splashed with blood. "Most of our Grenadiers and Light Infantry . . . lost three-fourths, and many nine-tenths, of their men," a British officer recalled. "Some had only eight and nine men in the company left, some only three, four, and five."

The British soldiers regrouped at the bottom of the hill. They advanced again and were forced back again, with many more men wounded and killed. As the battle raged, British warships began to bombard Charlestown, trying to drive out American snipers who were firing at the redcoats. Soon the whole town was ablaze, with flames leaping from the windows of nearly every house.

Across the river in Boston, thousands of spectators watched the battle from rooftops and hills. "Straight before us a large and noble town in one great blaze," wrote an observer. "The church steeples being of timber were great pyramids of fire above the rest. . . . The roar of cannon, mortars and musketry, the crash of churches, ships upon the stocks and whole streets falling together in ruins [filled] the air."

Evening shadows were falling when the reinforced redcoats finally threw off their heavy packs and, for the third time, advanced up the hill, stepping over the bodies of their fallen comrades. By then the rebels were running out of ammunition. The redcoats surged forward, plunged over the fortress walls, and after fierce hand-to-hand fighting, captured both Breed's Hill and Bunker Hill. "My God how the balls flew!" a militiaman remembered. "Four men were shot dead within five feet of me."

The British had taken the hills but paid a heavy price. "The dead lay as thick as sheep in a fold," said one combatant. More than a thousand British soldiers had been killed or wounded that afternoon—40 percent of the attacking force. The Americans had suffered nearly five hundred casualties. While they had been forced to give up their ground, they had crippled

Stepping over their fallen comrades, British troops march
in formation up Breed's Hill.

the British army in America and thrown it on the defensive. And they had
shown that, as free men, they could stand up to Europe's best soldiers.

George Washington was on his way north to take command of the
Continental Army when a courier met him on the road with news of the
Battle of Bunker Hill, as it came to be called. Soon afterward,
Washington made Cambridge his headquarters and began the task of
molding this spirited volunteer army into a disciplined military force.

The Continental Congress now had a real war on its hands but still no policy that everyone could agree on. More delegates had come around to the idea of independence, but others still resisted a formal break with England. On July 6, Congress approved a militant statement called "A Declaration of the Causes and Necessity of Taking up Arms" for Washington to read to his troops. It warned that the colonists would fight to preserve their liberties rather than submit to tyranny.

At the same time, the delegates also approved a new petition to King George, appealing once again for a peaceful reconciliation. It was called the Olive Branch Petition, because a branch from an olive tree is a traditional symbol of peace.

"We have . . . given Britain one more chance, one opportunity more, of recovering the friendship of the colonies," Benjamin Franklin wrote later, "which, however, I think she has not enough sense to embrace, and so I conclude she has lost them forever."

True to Franklin's prediction, when King George received the Olive Branch Petition in London, he refused to read it. He had already issued a royal proclamation, ordering that the American rebels be put down by force.

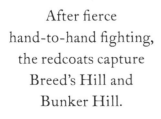

After fierce hand-to-hand fighting, the redcoats capture Breed's Hill and Bunker Hill.

7. Common Sense

For months after the Battle of Bunker Hill, British troops remained trapped in Boston as the rebels kept up their blockade. At his Cambridge headquarters, General George Washington pored over maps and studied intelligence reports, searching for weak points in the British defenses. At the same time, he tried to hide the sorry condition of his own ragged army.

The Americans were "neither armed nor clothed as they should be," Washington told his military secretary. "In short, my situation has been such that I have been obliged to conceal it from my own officers."

Clothing was in short supply because, in the past, most cloth had been imported from England. When it appeared that the blockade of Boston would last well into the winter, the rebels sent out an appeal for 13,000 winter coats.

George Washington takes command of the Continental Army at Cambridge, Massachusetts, in 1775.

That fall, in every colony, Patriot women worked at their spinning wheels and hand looms, making homespun coats for the Continental Army. Inside each coat, the maker sewed her name and the name of her town. Every soldier who volunteered for eight months' service received one of the coats, causing the British to sneer at Washington's troops as an army of "homespuns."

Washington had plenty to worry about. Along with a lack of supplies, he was plagued by a shortage of men. The Continental Congress had authorized an army of 20,000

A volunteer militiaman

well-armed troops, but as the blockade of Boston dragged on with little action on either side, Washington had trouble persuading his veterans to stay when their enlistments were up. By the beginning of 1776, his army was far below its authorized strength.

When Washington took command, there were many free blacks serving as volunteers in the Continental Army. African-American militiamen had fought valiantly at Lexington and Concord and at the Battle of Bunker Hill, where former slave Peter Salem received official commendation as "a brave and gallant soldier." Despite this bravery, southern delegates to the Continental Congress opposed the enlistment of blacks. The Southerners were afraid that giving guns and military training to black soldiers would encourage slave rebellions throughout the South.

Congress ordered Washington to stop recruiting blacks. Those already in the ranks could serve out their tour of duty, but no new blacks were to be accepted into the army. When the black soldiers protested, Washington wrote to the Congress, sympathizing with their complaints and asking for a clear-cut policy.

Early in 1776, Congress changed its decision and voted to admit free blacks into the ranks. Later, some states began to offer freedom to slaves in return for their service under arms. The adopted last names of some of these men—Jeffrey Liberty, Dick Freedom, Pomp Liberty—revealed why they were fighting. Eventually, about five thousand African-American volunteers from every state except Georgia and South Carolina served with the Continental Army. While there were several black regiments, most African Americans served in integrated units—the last integrated American army units until the Korean War in the 1950s.

The blockade of Boston continued for nearly eleven months. British and American patrols clashed whenever the rebels ventured too close to the British lines, but at first there was no serious fighting.

Impatient with the stalemate at Boston, the Continental Congress approved a daring plan to invade Canada and wrest that territory from British control. During the fall of 1775, an American expeditionary force commanded by General Richard Montgomery captured Montreal without much of a struggle. Montgomery then moved on to the fortress city of Quebec, where he joined a second American force, led by Benedict Arnold, that had marched north through the Maine wilderness.

Camped outside Quebec, the Americans waited for the first snowy night to launch their attack. At last, in the predawn darkness of December 31, during a snowfall that turned into a howling blizzard, they stormed the city's

The attack on Quebec

immense walls with scaling ladders. Montgomery and two of his aides were shot down instantly, and the rest of his men were thrown back with heavy losses. About sixty American soldiers lost their lives that night; more than four hundred were taken prisoner. The survivors hunkered down outside the city under Arnold's command. There they remained, waiting for reinforcements, throughout the brutal Canadian winter.

Far to the south in Virginia, the British lost a battle when five hundred American militiamen forced them to evacuate the important seaport of Norfolk. Three weeks later, British warships retaliated. On New Year's Day, 1776, they bombarded Norfolk from the sea, starting a blaze that lasted fifty hours and burned the town to the ground.

Meanwhile, at his headquarters in Cambridge, George Washington was planning a showdown with the British. In the middle of January, ox teams arrived in Cambridge hauling cannons and mortars that had been captured from the British at Fort Ticonderoga and dragged three hundred miles across the snow-covered hills of western Massachusetts. The guns were repaired and made serviceable, and on the night of March 4, Washington's troops took possession of Dorchester Heights, just south of Boston. Working quickly under cover of darkness—just as they had on Breed's Hill months before—the Americans built fortifications. But this time they had their new artillery, and by daybreak, the big guns were in place. The rebels were now in a position to destroy Boston and its British garrison.

"My God! These fellows have done more work in one night than I could make my army do in three months," exclaimed the British commander General William Howe. He sent out a flag of truce and offered to evacuate the city peacefully, provided his own troops were not attacked as they left. Washington agreed to keep the rebel guns silent. On March 17, the British forces sailed away from Boston in a flotilla of 170 warships, transports, and schooners, taking with them more than a thousand Loyalists—Americans who had sworn an oath of allegiance to

The British evacuation of Boston

King George and were now unhappy refugees.

"The more I think of [it]," Abigail Adams wrote to her husband, John, "the more amazed I am that they should leave such a harbor, such fortifications, such entrenchments, and that we should be in peaceable possession of a town which we expected would cost us a river of blood."

The Revolutionary War had been going on for nearly a year, but so far nothing had been settled. The Continental Congress was still meeting in Philadelphia, and still debating.

Americans, meanwhile, had been reading a powerful argument in favor of independence. Thomas Paine's *Common Sense*, first published in January 1776, worked "a wonderful change in the minds of many men," as George Washington said. In stirring language that ordinary people could easily understand, Paine argued that the American colonies would have to make a complete break with England.

Though he had little formal education, Paine was a masterful writer. Born in England, he ran away to sea at the age of sixteen, worked at many jobs, schooled himself, and wound up in London, where he met Ben Franklin. Impressed by Paine's talents, Franklin urged him to emigrate to America. Paine arrived in Philadelphia in 1774, found work as a magazine editor, and soon began writing his influential pamphlet.

He didn't waste time blaming Parliament or the king's advisers for the troubles in America. He put the blame squarely on King George III, that "Royal Brute of England," a "tyrant" who had sent soldiers against his own subjects. And he denounced the very idea of monarchy, calling it a tyrannical form of government. "Of more worth is one honest man to society, and in the sight of God, than all the crowned ruffians that ever lived," he wrote.

Paine urged the American colonists to rebel against the British monarchy, to throw off that tyranny and proclaim their independence. He fired off some practical arguments. England was a small island and had no business trying to rule an entire continent three thousand miles away. British taxes and trade restrictions were harming rather than helping the colonies. But above all, Paine appealed to the colonists' longing for self-government. People have a right to govern themselves, he argued. The time had come to exercise that right.

America had a mission in the world as the champion of liberty, Paine declared. Unburdened by a monarchy or by hereditary privilege, which had oppressed the peoples of the Old World, America was the place where universal freedom could take root and flourish.

Benjamin Blyth's portrait of Abigail Adams. Her letters to her husband, John, when he was away at the Continental Congress, are a revealing source of information about the issues, events, and personalities of the Revolutionary War era. Though (like other women of the time) Abigail had no formal schooling, she read widely and spoke her mind freely.

Thomas Paine, author of *Common Sense*

THE HORSE AMERICA, *throwing his Master.*

This British cartoon depicts rebellious America (the horse) throwing off English rule (the rider, King George III).

"The cause of America is in a great measure the cause of all mankind," he wrote. "We have it in our power to begin the world again."

Common Sense said in plain language what many colonists felt in their hearts, and it had a tremendous impact on public opinion. It went through twenty-five editions in 1776 and sold more than 150,000 copies in America alone. In proportion to the population at that time, it still ranks as the greatest best-seller in American history. The pamphlet "struck a string which required but a touch to make it vibrate," said the Reverend Ashbel Green. "The country was ripe for independence and only needed somebody to tell the people so, with decision, boldness, and plausibility."

The Continental Congress had been moving gradually toward independence, and the enormous popularity of *Common Sense* pushed the delegates closer to a final break with England. Stubborn King George wasn't helping his own cause. Congress learned that he had recruited 18,000 German mercenaries for his army and was releasing convicts from prison if they agreed to fight in America.

Meanwhile, the British were trying to incite Indian attacks on border settlements. They were encouraging slave revolts in the South with false promises of emancipation. And British warships were still bombarding American towns along the coast.

By May 1776, Congress was referring to the colonies as "states" and was urging those states to form governments independent of Britain. One after another, the states were drafting resolutions in favor of independence. Finally, on June 7, Richard Henry Lee of Virginia rose in Congress to offer this momentous resolution:

> "That these United Colonies are, and of right ought to be, free and independent States, that they are absolved from all allegiance to the British Crown, and that all political connection between them and the State of Great Britain is, and ought to be, totally dissolved."

Lee's motion was seconded by John Adams. It was supported by seven of the state delegations. The other six—New York, New Jersey, Pennsylvania, Delaware, Maryland, and South Carolina—held back.

After two days of debate, the delegates agreed to delay a vote on Lee's resolution for three weeks, until July 1, so that they could write home for instructions from their state governments. "Some among us urge strongly for Independence and eternal separation," Joseph Hewes of North Carolina told a friend, "while others wish to wait a little longer and to have the opinion of their constituents."

Congress then appointed a committee to draw up a statement explaining why the colonies would be justified in declaring themselves independent—just in case such a declaration would be needed. The committee members were Roger Sherman of Connecticut, John Adams of Massachusetts, Benjamin Franklin of Pennsylvania, Robert R. Livingston of New York, and Thomas Jefferson of Virginia.

Richard Henry Lee of Virginia proposed a resolution in the Continental Congress calling for independence from Great Britain.

8. Declaring Independence: *July 4, 1776*

At age thirty-three, Thomas Jefferson was one of the youngest delegates to the Continental Congress. A tall, slim, quiet man with gray eyes and reddish hair, he could be lively and even vivacious among his friends. But in public he was so reserved, so soft-spoken and shy, he often seemed stiff or aloof. "During the whole time I sat with him in the Congress," said John Adams, "I never heard him utter three sentences together."

Though Jefferson did not say much, he was an avid scholar and an accomplished writer. Ever since his student days, he had practiced writing by condensing everything he read, striving to develop what he considered "the most valuable of all the talents, that of never using two words when one will do."

Adams wanted Jefferson to write the first draft of the statement we know today as the Declaration of Independence—a tough job, since the writer would have to come up with a document that all thirteen colonies could accept.

It seems that Jefferson tried to get out of the assignment. He wanted Adams to write the first draft. But Adams refused. Years later Adams recalled the following conversation:

"You should do it," said Jefferson.

"Oh, no!"

"Why will you not?"

"I will not."

"Why?" pressed Jefferson.

"Reasons enough," said Adams.

"What can be your reasons?"

"Reason, first, you are a Virginian and a Virginian ought to appear at the head of this business. Reason second, I am obnoxious, suspected and unpopular. You are very much otherwise. Reason third, you can write ten times better than I can."

So it was settled. Jefferson went to work in his rented rooms on the second floor of a brick house at the corner of Market and Seventh Streets in downtown Philadelphia.

The Committee for Drafting the Declaration of Independence: Benjamin Franklin, Thomas Jefferson, John Adams, Robert R. Livingston, Roger Sherman

Every morning he would rise before dawn, soak his feet in a basin of cold water, have tea and biscuits, then sit down at a small portable desk he had designed himself and start writing.

"I did not consider it part of my charge to invent new ideas," he said later, "but to place before mankind the common sense of the subject."

There were plenty of ideas in the air for Jefferson to draw on. He was familiar with the writings of John Locke, an influential English philosopher who argued that people are born with certain natural rights and that governments should be run for the benefit of everyone, not just for their rulers. Like most Americans, Jefferson had read Thomas Paine's *Common Sense* and other revolutionary pamphlets. A number of state and local governments, including Virginia's, had already issued declarations of rights and resolutions on independence that could serve as his models.

Scratching away with his quill pen, he worked on the Declaration for about two weeks while attending daily meetings of the Congress—constantly writing and rewriting, ripping up his earlier drafts as he made changes. On one draft that still exists, he changed nearly one third of the words. Finally he showed his work to John Adams and Ben Franklin, who suggested additional changes before the draft was submitted to Congress on June 28.

While Jefferson worked on his many drafts, news reached Philadelphia that British warships had bombarded Charleston, South Carolina, the South's most important seaport. A large British fleet had also been sighted off New York. And there was terrible news from Canada, where the invading Americans had been forced to retreat in total disorder, suffering from smallpox, malaria, and dysentery. Some five thousand American troops had been killed or wounded during the disastrous ten-month Canadian campaign.

With these alarming reports as a background, Congress began its final debate on independence. Before the delegates could consider Jefferson's declaration, they had to vote on Richard Henry Lee's resolution stating "That these United Colonies are, and of right ought to be, free and independent States."

On the steamy afternoon of July 1, John Dickinson of Pennsylvania rose to speak for the moderates. His voice trembled with emotion as he warned the dele-

An artist's impression of Thomas Jefferson working on the Declaration of Independence by candlelight

gates that independence was risky and premature. To abandon the protection of Great Britain would be "like destroying our house in winter and exposing a growing family before we have got another shelter." He argued that a way must be found to get along with England.

As John Adams began his reply, a summer storm crackled and exploded in the heavens above Philadelphia. Thunder shook the statehouse windows and lightning flashed against the darkening sky while Adams pleaded the cause of independence. No record of his words exists, but Jefferson remembered that Adams spoke "with a power of thought and expression that moved us from our seats."

When the vote was taken, only nine colonies voted for independence. Pennsylvania and South Carolina were opposed. Delaware's two delegates were divided. And New

An early draft of the Declaration of Independence showing Jefferson's handwritten revisions

York's delegates abstained, saying they had no instructions from home.

The delegates who favored independence got busy behind the scenes. After a night of intense negotiations, Pennsylvania and South Carolina agreed to change their votes and go along with the other colonies. An absent Delaware delegate, Caesar Rodney, who also favored independence, rode eighty miles through heavy rain to reach Philadelphia and break the tie in his delegation's vote. New York, still lacking instructions, abstained again.

The final vote on July 2 was twelve colonies in favor of independence, none opposed. Two weeks later, New York's delegates were able to add their colony's approval, making the vote for independence unanimous.

Congress then turned to the wording of Jefferson's draft. During a three-day period, from late Tuesday, July 2, through Thursday, July 4, the delegates went over the document word by word. Jefferson, justly proud of his composition, squirmed in his seat, listening in unhappy silence as whole paragraphs were taken out, as new words and phrases were added. In all, nearly one hundred changes were made. Jefferson's text was cut by about a fourth. John Adams believed that Congress worked some real improvements into the text, but also "obliterated some of the best of it."

The most hotly contested change concerned a long passage Jefferson had written attacking the slave trade and blaming King George III for imposing slavery on America. Jefferson himself lived in a slave society. He owned more than two hundred slaves. His plantations and way of life depended on the labors of the human property he had inherited. Yet he

Jefferson supervising a slave at work

considered slavery an evil that should gradually be abolished. More than once, he had proposed plans to end the slave trade in Virginia. In his draft of the Declaration, he denounced slavery as "a cruel war against human nature itself, violating its most sacred rights of life and liberty."

At that time in America, it was easier to denounce slavery than to put an end to it. Southern slave owners in the Continental Congress, particularly those from Georgia and South Carolina, refused to sign a document that included Jefferson's tough anti-slavery passage. They "had never attempted to restrain the importation of slaves," Jefferson wrote later, but "still wished to continue it." The Southerners were backed by some of the delegates from New England, whose merchants had grown rich shipping slaves from Africa to the colonies. "For though their people had very few slaves themselves," said Jefferson, "yet they had been pretty considerable carriers of them to others."

John Adams, Ben Franklin, and other revolutionary leaders had spoken out strongly against slavery, but for the sake of unity, they agreed to compromise. The anti-slavery passage was eliminated. The explosive question of slavery was put aside and would not be resolved until America's Civil War nearly a century later.

Jefferson continued to denounce "this abominable crime" of slavery and to propose plans for the eventual emancipation of all slaves. "Nothing is more certainly written in the book of fate, than that these people are to be free," he wrote. And yet he was not exempt from the prejudices shared by so many of his fellow white colonists. Jefferson believed that African Americans could never take their place in American society. He suggested that they should be relocated elsewhere once they were freed, perhaps back to Africa—a view held by many others at that time. And he remained a slave owner throughout his life. Recent evidence suggests that Jefferson may have fathered several children with his slave Sally Hemings, who lived for many years as a member of Jefferson's household.

Jefferson and his fellow committee members presenting the Declaration
of Independence to John Hancock, president of the Continental Congress

On July 4, 1776, swarms of horseflies from a nearby stable invaded the
assembly room, encouraging the delegates to bring their deliberations to a
close. The final version of the Declaration of Independence was voted on
and approved unanimously. As soon as the vote was taken, a boy stationed
at the statehouse door began to clap his hands and shout, "Ring! Ring!" At
nearby Christ's Church, the old bellman was waiting for that signal.

That afternoon, the Declaration of Independence was signed by John
Hancock, president of the Continental Congress. He said he would
make his signature large enough so that King George would be able to
read it without his glasses. Most historians believe that no other signatures were added until August 2, after the document had been copied
onto a sheet of durable parchment, when every member present signed

it. The remaining members added their signatures at later times.

One signer, Stephen Hopkins of Rhode Island, had a condition called palsy that caused his hands to shake. As he took up his pen to add his name to the Declaration, he said, "My hand trembles, but my heart does not."

Each man among them knew that by signing the Declaration of Independence, he had become a traitor to England. If captured by the British, he could pay with his life. The outcome of the Revolutionary War would decide whether the signers would be remembered as the founders of a nation or be hanged by the British for treason.

Meanwhile, copies of the Declaration were printed and carried by express riders and coastal schooners to towns and vil-

John Hancock was the first to sign. He wrote his name in a large, bold hand, "so the King doesn't have to put on his spectacles."

lages in each of the thirteen states, where the text was read aloud amid "great demonstrations of joy." General George Washington and his troops heard it read in New York City on July 9. That evening a jubilant crowd pulled down a fifteen-foot-high gilded statue of George III on horseback. Later, the statue was melted down and the metal molded into 42,000 bullets for Patriot guns.

Pulling down the statue of King George III in New York City

9. Your Rights and Mine

Although many changes were made to it by Congress, the Declaration of Independence remained essentially Thomas Jefferson's creation. Jefferson began by stating the purpose of the document: to explain why the colonies had voted to free themselves from British rule. "All men are created equal," Jefferson wrote. They have certain God-given rights, including the rights to "Life, Liberty and the pursuit of Happiness." And governments are created to secure those rights.

Jefferson then charged that King George III had repeatedly violated the colonists' rights, his purpose being "the establishment of an absolute Tyranny over these States." He gave a long list of examples, including "imposing Taxes on us without our Consent," "depriving us in many cases, of the benefits of Trial by Jury," "suspending our own Legislatures," and "waging War against us."

Today, Jefferson's indictment of King

A public reading of the Declaration of Independence

George as a tyrant may seem like ancient history. But the preamble to the Declaration, the opening statement, is recognized as a timeless affirmation of human rights and representative government.

Governments must have "the consent of the governed," Jefferson wrote. Whenever any government fails to protect the rights of its citizens, the citizens have the right to change it or to abolish it and to create a new government. That powerful idea has inspired popular resistance to tyranny in countries all over the world.

One measure of the Declaration's lasting influence is that the values it expresses have taken on expanded meanings with the passage of time. More than two centuries ago, when Jefferson wrote that "all men are created equal," few people gave much thought to women's rights. Women were shut out of public life. They did not vote, hold office, or even attend town meetings. Jefferson did not mention women in any of his drafts. Later he wrote that American women were "too wise to wrinkle their foreheads with politics."

Did Jefferson, a slave owner, mean to include black men when he wrote "all men are created equal" and endowed with "certain unalienable Rights"? In colonial America, enslaved Africans had no rights at all. Yet Jefferson knew that slavery was wrong, and he said so in the long passage of his declaration that denounced the slave trade. That passage was eliminated, but the idea of *equality* remained embedded in the Declaration of Independence; and as American history unfolded, that was the idea that prevailed.

During the 1780s, 1790s, and early 1800s, the lofty ideas expressed in the Declaration of Independence led northern states to free slaves within their borders. And in 1848, women's rights advocates meeting at Seneca Falls, New York, drafted a Declaration of Sentiments based on the Declaration of Independence; they proclaimed that "all men and women are created equal."

Abraham Lincoln believed that the Declaration of Independence expressed the highest political truths in history. He said that blacks and

Celebrating the Fourth of July. In towns, villages, and country hamlets
across the land, people raised liberty poles, rang bells, fired guns and cannons,
built bonfires, marched in parades, played games and sports, and put on shows
as they observed Independence Day.

whites alike were entitled to the rights it spelled out. Lincoln regarded
equal rights as an *ideal*, a set of goals to be "constantly looked to, and constantly labored for, even though never perfectly attained . . . augmenting
the happiness and value of life to all people of all colors everywhere."

The signers of the Declaration of Independence did not mean that all
men are "equal in all respects," said Lincoln. People differ greatly in
intelligence, strength, talent, character, and many other attributes. What
the signers stated in "plain, unmistakable language," Lincoln insisted,
was that all men are equal in having " 'certain inalienable rights.'. . . This
they said, and this they meant."

They had no intention of affirming the "obvious untruth, that all were then enjoying that equality," Lincoln continued. The signers meant "simply to declare the *right* so that the *enforcement* of it might follow as fast as the circumstances should permit."

Lincoln pointed out that Americans could have declared independence from England without ever mentioning equality and unalienable rights. But they chose "to introduce into a merely revolutionary document, an abstract truth, applicable to all men and all times."

In 1963, a century after Lincoln signed the Emancipation Proclamation, Martin Luther King, Jr., stood on the steps of the Lincoln Memorial in Washington, D.C., and proclaimed his dream that Americans of all races would one day live in harmony: "It is a dream deeply rooted in the American dream, that one day this nation will rise up and live out the true meaning of its creed—we hold these truths to be self-evident, that all men are created equal."

Like Lincoln, King regarded the Declaration of Independence as a living document that speaks anew to each generation. Here is the passage that most people remember and that is inscribed, in part, on the Jefferson Memorial in Washington, D.C.:

We hold these truths to be self-evident, that all men are created equal, that they are endowed by their Creator with certain unalienable Rights, that among these are Life, Liberty and the pursuit of Happiness.— That to secure these rights, Governments are instituted among Men, deriving their just powers from the consent of the governed,—That whenever any Form of Government becomes destructive of these ends, it is the Right of the People to alter or to abolish it, and to institute new Government, laying its foundation on such principles and organizing its powers in such form, as to them shall seem most likely to effect their Safety and Happiness.

IN CONGRESS, JULY 4, 1776.

The unanimous Declaration of the thirteen united States of America.

When in the Course of human events, it becomes necessary for one people to dissolve the political bands which have connected them with another, and to assume among the powers of the earth, the separate and equal station to which the Laws of Nature and of Nature's God entitle them, a decent respect to the opinions of mankind requires that they should declare the causes which impel them to the separation.

We hold these truths to be self-evident, that all men are created equal, that they are endowed by their Creator with certain unalienable Rights, that among these are Life, Liberty and the pursuit of Happiness. — That to secure these rights, Governments are instituted among Men, deriving their just powers from the consent of the governed, — That whenever any Form of Government becomes destructive of these ends, it is the Right of the People to alter or to abolish it, and to institute new Government, laying its foundation on such principles and organizing its powers in such form, as to them shall seem most likely to effect their Safety and Happiness. Prudence, indeed, will dictate that Governments long established should not be changed for light and transient causes; and accordingly all experience hath shewn, that mankind are more disposed to suffer, while evils are sufferable, than to right themselves by abolishing the forms to which they are accustomed. But when a long train of abuses and usurpations, pursuing invariably the same Object evinces a design to reduce them under absolute Despotism, it is their right, it is their duty, to throw off such Government, and to provide new Guards for their future security. — Such has been the patient sufferance of these Colonies; and such is now the necessity which constrains them to alter their former Systems of Government. The history of the present King of Great Britain is a history of repeated injuries and usurpations, all having in direct object the establishment of an absolute Tyranny over these States. To prove this, let Facts be submitted to a candid world.

He has refused his Assent to Laws, the most wholesome and necessary for the public good.

He has forbidden his Governors to pass Laws of immediate and pressing importance, unless suspended in their operation till his Assent should be obtained; and when so suspended, he has utterly neglected to attend to them.

He has refused to pass other Laws for the accommodation of large districts of people, unless those people would relinquish the right of Representation in the Legislature, a right inestimable to them and formidable to tyrants only.

He has called together legislative bodies at places unusual, uncomfortable, and distant from the depository of their public Records, for the sole purpose of fatiguing them into compliance with his measures.

He has dissolved Representative Houses repeatedly, for opposing with manly firmness his invasions on the rights of the people.

He has refused for a long time, after such dissolutions, to cause others to be elected; whereby the Legislative powers, incapable of Annihilation, have returned to the People at large for their exercise; the State remaining in the mean time exposed to all the dangers of invasion from without, and convulsions within.

He has endeavoured to prevent the population of these States; for that purpose obstructing the Laws for Naturalization of Foreigners; refusing to pass others to encourage their migrations hither, and raising the conditions of new Appropriations of Lands.

He has obstructed the Administration of Justice, by refusing his Assent to Laws for establishing Judiciary powers.

He has made Judges dependent on his Will alone, for the tenure of their offices, and the amount and payment of their salaries.

He has erected a multitude of New Offices, and sent hither swarms of Officers to harrass our people, and eat out their substance.

He has kept among us, in times of peace, Standing Armies without the Consent of our legislatures.

He has affected to render the Military independent of and superior to the Civil power.

He has combined with others to subject us to a jurisdiction foreign to our constitution, and unacknowledged by our laws; giving his Assent to their Acts of pretended Legislation:

For Quartering large bodies of armed troops among us: — For protecting them, by a mock Trial, from punishment for any Murders which they should commit on the Inhabitants of these States: — For cutting off our Trade with all parts of the world: — For imposing Taxes on us without our Consent: — For depriving us in many cases, of the benefits of Trial by jury: — For transporting us beyond Seas to be tried for pretended offences: — For abolishing the free System of English Laws in a neighbouring Province, establishing therein an Arbitrary government, and enlarging its Boundaries so as to render it at once an example and fit instrument for introducing the same absolute rule into these Colonies: — For taking away our Charters, abolishing our most valuable Laws, and altering fundamentally the Forms of our Governments: — For suspending our own Legislatures, and declaring themselves invested with power to legislate for us in all cases whatsoever.

He has abdicated Government here, by declaring us out of his Protection and waging War against us.

He has plundered our seas, ravaged our Coasts, burnt our towns, and destroyed the lives of our people.

He is at this time transporting large Armies of foreign Mercenaries to compleat the works of death, desolation and tyranny, already begun with circumstances of Cruelty & perfidy scarcely paralleled in the most barbarous ages, and totally unworthy the Head of a civilized nation.

He has constrained our fellow Citizens taken Captive on the high Seas to bear Arms against their country, to become the executioners of their friends and Brethren, or to fall themselves by their Hands.

He has excited domestic insurrections amongst us, and has endeavoured to bring on the inhabitants of our frontiers, the merciless Indian Savages, whose known rule of warfare, is an undistinguished destruction of all ages, sexes and conditions.

In every stage of these Oppressions We have Petitioned for Redress in the most humble terms: Our repeated Petitions have been answered only by repeated injury. A Prince, whose character is thus marked by every act which may define a Tyrant, is unfit to be the ruler of a free people.

Nor have We been wanting in attentions to our Brittish brethren. We have warned them from time to time of attempts by their legislature to extend an unwarrantable jurisdiction over us. We have reminded them of the circumstances of our emigration and settlement here. We have appealed to their native justice and magnanimity, and we have conjured them by the ties of our common kindred to disavow these usurpations, which, would inevitably interrupt our connections and correspondence. They too have been deaf to the voice of justice and of consanguinity. We must, therefore, acquiesce in the necessity, which denounces our Separation, and hold them, as we hold the rest of mankind, Enemies in War, in Peace Friends.

We, therefore, the Representatives of the united States of America, in General Congress, Assembled, appealing to the Supreme Judge of the world for the rectitude of our intentions, do, in the Name, and by Authority of the good People of these Colonies, solemnly publish and declare, That these United Colonies are, and of Right ought to be Free and Independent States; that they are Absolved from all Allegiance to the British Crown, and that all political connection between them and the State of Great Britain, is and ought to be totally dissolved; and that as Free and Independent States, they have full Power to levy War, conclude Peace, contract Alliances, establish Commerce, and to do all other Acts and Things which Independent States may of right do. — And for the support of this Declaration, with a firm reliance on the protection of Divine Providence, we mutually pledge to each other our Lives, our Fortunes and our sacred Honor.

John Hancock

Button Gwinnett
Lyman Hall
Geo Walton.

Wm Hooper
Joseph Hewes,
John Penn

Edward Rutledge.

Thos Heyward Junr.
Thomas Lynch Junr.
Arthur Middleton

Samuel Chase
Wm Paca
Thos. Stone
Charles Carroll of Carrollton

George Wythe
Richard Henry Lee
Th Jefferson
Benja Harrison
Thos Nelson jr.
Francis Lightfoot Lee
Carter Braxton

Robt Morris
Benjamin Rush
Benja. Franklin
John Morton
Geo Clymer
Jas. Smith
Geo. Taylor
James Wilson
Geo. Ross
Caesar Rodney
Geo Read
Tho M:Kean

Wm Floyd
Phil. Livingston
Frans. Lewis
Lewis Morris

Richd Stockton
Jno Witherspoon
Fras. Hopkinson
John Hart
Abra Clark

Josiah Bartlett
Wm Whipple
Saml Adams
John Adams
Robt Treat Paine
Elbridge Gerry
Step Hopkins
William Ellery
Roger Sherman
Sam el Huntington
Wm Williams
Oliver Wolcott
Matthew Thornton

The Declaration of Independence

In CONGRESS, July 4, 1776.

The unanimous Declaration of the thirteen united States of America,

When in the Course of human events it becomes necessary for one people to dissolve the political bands which have connected them with another, and to assume among the powers of the earth, the separate and equal station to which the Laws of Nature and of Nature's God entitle them, a decent respect to the opinions of mankind requires that they should declare the causes which impel them to the separation.

We hold these truths to be self-evident, that all men are created equal, that they are endowed by their Creator with certain unalienable Rights, that among these are Life, Liberty and the pursuit of Happiness.—That to secure these rights, Governments are instituted among Men, deriving their just powers from the consent of the governed,—That whenever any Form of Government becomes destructive of these ends, it is the Right of the People to alter or to abolish it, and to institute new Government, laying its foundation on such principles and organizing its powers in such form, as to them shall seem most likely to effect their Safety and Happiness. Prudence, indeed, will dictate that Governments long established should not be changed for light and transient causes; and accordingly all experience hath shewn, that mankind are more disposed to suffer, while evils are sufferable, than to right themselves by abolishing the forms to which they are accustomed. But when a long train of abuses and usurpations, pursuing invariably the same Object evinces a design to reduce them under absolute Despotism, it is their right, it is their duty, to throw off such Government, and to provide new Guards for their future security.—Such has been the patient sufferance of these Colonies; and such is now the necessity which constrains them to alter their former Systems of Government. The history of the present King of Great Britain is a history of repeated injuries and usurpations, all having in direct object the establishment of an absolute Tyranny over these States. To prove this, let Facts be submitted to a candid world.

He has refused his Assent to Laws, the most wholesome and necessary for the public good.

He has forbidden his Governors to pass Laws of immediate and pressing importance, unless suspended in their operation till his Assent should be obtained; and when so suspended, he has utterly neglected to attend to them.

He has refused to pass other Laws for the accommodation of large districts of people, unless those people would relinquish the right of Representation in the Legislature, a right inestimable to them and formidable to tyrants only.

He has called together legislative bodies at places unusual, uncomfortable, and distant from the depository of their Public Records, for the sole purpose of fatiguing them into compliance with his measures.

He has dissolved Representative Houses repeatedly, for opposing with manly firmness his invasions on the rights of the people.

He has refused for a long time, after such dissolutions, to cause others to be elected; whereby the Legislative powers, incapable of Annihilation, have returned to the People at large for their exercise; the State remaining in the mean time exposed to all the dangers of invasion from without, and convulsions within.

He has endeavoured to prevent the population of these States; for that purpose obstructing the Laws for Naturalization of Foreigners; refusing to pass others to encourage their migrations hither, and raising the conditions of new Appropriations of Lands.

He has obstructed the Administration of Justice, by refusing his Assent to Laws for establishing Judiciary Powers.

He has made Judges dependent on his Will alone, for the tenure of their offices, and the amount and payment of their salaries.

He has erected a multitude of New Offices, and sent hither swarms of Officers to harass our people, and eat out their substance.

He has kept among us, in times of peace, Standing Armies without the Consent of our legislatures.

He has affected to render the Military independent of and superior to the Civil power.

He has combined with others to subject us to a jurisdiction foreign to our constitution, and unacknowledged by our laws; giving his Assent to their Acts of pretended Legislation:

For quartering large bodies of armed troops among us:

For protecting them, by a mock Trial, from punishment for any Murders which they should commit on the Inhabitants of these States:

For cutting off our Trade with all parts of the world:

For imposing Taxes on us without our Consent:

For depriving us in many cases, of the benefits of Trial by Jury:

For transporting us beyond Seas to be tried for pretended offences:

For abolishing the free System of English Laws in a neighbouring Province, establishing therein an Arbitrary government, and enlarging its Boundaries so as to render it at once an example and fit instrument for introducing the same absolute rule into these Colonies:

For taking away our Charters, abolishing our most valuable Laws, and altering fundamentally the Forms of our Governments:

For suspending our own Legislatures, and declaring themselves invested with power to legislate for us in all cases whatsoever.

He has abdicated Government here, by declaring us out of his Protection and waging War against us.

He has plundered our seas, ravaged our Coasts, burnt our towns, and destroyed the lives of our people.

He is at this time transporting large Armies of foreign Mercenaries to compleat the works of death, desolation and tyranny, already begun with circumstances of Cruelty & perfidy scarcely paralleled in the most barbarous ages, and totally unworthy the Head of a civilized nation.

He has constrained our fellow Citizens taken Captive on the high Seas to bear Arms against their Country, to become the executioners of their friends and Brethren, or to fall themselves by their Hands.

He has excited domestic insurrections amongst us, and has endeavoured to bring on the inhabitants of our frontiers, the merciless Indian Savages, whose known rule of warfare, is an undistinguished destruction of all ages, sexes and conditions.

In every stage of these Oppressions We have Petitioned for Redress in the most humble terms: Our repeated Petitions have been answered only by repeated injury. A Prince, whose character is thus marked by every act which may define a Tyrant, is unfit to be the ruler of a free people. Nor have We been wanting in attentions to our Brittish brethren. We have warned them from time to time of attempts by their legislature to extend an unwarrantable jurisdiction over us. We have reminded them of the circumstances of our emigration and settlement here. We have appealed to their native justice and magnanimity, and we have conjured them by the ties of our common kindred to disavow these usurpations, which would inevitably interrupt our connections and correspondence. They too have been deaf to the voice of justice and of consanguinity. We must, therefore, acquiesce in the necessity, which denounces our Separation, and hold them, as we hold the rest of mankind, Enemies in War, in Peace Friends.—

We, therefore, the Representatives of the united States of America, in General Congress, Assembled, appealing to the Supreme Judge of the world for the rectitude of our intentions, do, in the Name, and by Authority of the good People of these Colonies, solemnly publish and declare, That these United Colonies are, and of Right ought to be Free and Independent States; that they are Absolved from all Allegiance to the British Crown, and that all political connection between them and the State of Great Britain, is and ought to be totally dissolved; and that as Free and Independent States, they have full

Power to levy War, conclude Peace, contract Alliances, establish Commerce, and to do all other Acts and Things which Independent States may of right do. —And for the support of this Declaration, with a firm reliance on the protection of Divine Providence, we mutually pledge to each other our Lives, our Fortunes and our sacred Honor.

John Hancock

Button Gwinnett

Lyman Hall

Geo. Walton

Wm. Hooper

Joseph Hewes

John Penn

Edward Rutledge

Thos. Heyward, Jr.

Thomas Lynch, Jr.

Arthur Middleton

Samuel Chase

Wm. Paca

Thos. Stone

Charles Carroll of Carrollton

George Wythe

Richard Henry Lee

Th. Jefferson

Benj. Harrison

Thos. Nelson, Jr.

Francis Lightfoot Lee

Carter Braxton

Robt. Morris

Benjamin Rush

Benj. Franklin

John Morton

Geo. Clymer

Jas. Smith

Geo. Taylor

James Wilson

Geo. Ross

Caesar Rodney

Geo. Read

Tho. M:Kean

Wm. Floyd

Phil. Livingston

Frans. Lewis

Lewis Morris

Richd. Stockton

Jno. Witherspoon

Fras. Hopkinson

John Hart

Abra. Clark

Josiah Bartlett

Wm. Whipple

Saml. Adams

John Adams

Robt. Treat Paine

Elbridge Gerry

Step. Hopkins

William Ellery

Roger Sherman

Sam. Huntington

Wm. Williams

Oliver Wolcott

Matthew Thornton

Visiting the Declaration of Independence

In 1776, after the Declaration of Independence was approved, it was copied onto a sheet of parchment and signed by delegates to the Second Continental Congress. Since then, the document has been battered, bandaged, and abused. It has been hauled from place to place; exposed to the harmful effects of light, heat, and humidity; and rescued more than once from the perils of war.

During the Revolutionary War, as the Continental Congress kept moving to escape the British, the Declaration was probably rolled up, as was customary with parchment scrolls, and was carried along with other important papers. During the War of 1812, when the British marched into Washington and burned the White House, a government clerk saved the document from destruction by spiriting it away to Leesburg, Virginia, where it was safely hidden.

When the United States entered World War II in 1941, the Declaration was packed in an elaborate container and sent to the U.S. depository at Fort Knox, Kentucky, where the nation's gold bullion is stored. The document traveled to Kentucky in a special train, escorted by armed Secret Service agents and troops of the Thirteenth Armored Division.

Over the years, meanwhile, the document has been transferred from one government building to another. In the days before air-conditioning and climate control, it was subjected to great variations of temperature and humidity. In 1841, when it was put on public display for the first time, it was hung on a wall in the new Patent Office Building opposite a large window, where it remained, exposed to sunlight, for thirty-five years.

By the time the document was a century old, it was showing alarming signs of deterioration. The parchment, made from animal skin, was marked by tears, cracks, and bends. The edges had curled. And the black iron-based ink with which the founding fathers had signed their names was fading to brown.

Scientists were called in to examine the document, and they began to recommend measures to preserve it. To start with, it was shielded from light. Eventually it was placed in the high-tech protective case it occupies today, where it is monitored and tended by experts skilled in modern conservation technology.

The Declaration of Independence is on display in the rotunda of the National Archives Building in Washington, D.C., along with the U.S. Constitution and the Bill of Rights. The three documents are enclosed for public viewing in massive, bronze-framed, bulletproof glass containers, filled with inert helium gas to displace damaging oxygen, and with water vapor to keep the parchment from becoming brittle. The containers are equipped with an electronic device to detect helium loss, and the documents themselves are scanned regularly with a computerized imaging system.

At night, the containers are lowered into a vault of reinforced concrete and steel that is 22 feet deep and weighs 55 tons. Once the documents are safely inside the vault, the massive doors on top are swung shut. A working model on display in the rotunda shows how the containers are mechanically lowered into the vault.

Also on display are other historic documents, including journals kept during the Continental Congress; a letter from George Washington reporting the victory at Yorktown; a copy of the Treaty of Paris, which ended the Revolutionary War; and an early version of England's Magna Carta of 1215, the distant original ancestor of America's Declaration of Independence.

The Declaration of Independence may also be viewed on the website of the National Archives at:

http://www.nara.gov/exhall/charters/declaration/decmain.html

Chronology of Events

1607:	Jamestown settled
1620:	The Pilgrims land at Plymouth
1763:	The Treaty of Paris ends the French and Indian War
1765:	Parliament passes the Stamp Act, imposing taxes on all printed matter issued in the American colonies; the Sons of Liberty demonstrate against taxation without representation
1766:	Parliament repeals the Stamp Act
1767:	Parliament passes the Townshend Acts, taxing tea and other goods
MARCH 5, 1770:	British soldiers kill five Americans in the Boston Massacre; Parliament repeals all Townshend duties except those on tea
DECEMBER 16, 1773:	Patriots destroy 342 chests of tea at the Boston Tea Party
MARCH 24, 1774:	Parliament passes the Intolerable Acts
JUNE 1, 1774:	Blockade of Boston Harbor takes effect
SEPTEMBER 1774:	The First Continental Congress meets in Philadelphia
APRIL 19, 1775:	The battles of Lexington and Concord; Patriots blockade British-occupied Boston
MAY 1775:	The Second Continental Congress meets in Philadelphia; American volunteers led by Ethan Allen and Benedict Arnold capture Fort Ticonderoga
JUNE 15, 1775:	George Washington appointed commander of American forces
JUNE 17, 1775:	The battle of Breed's Hill and Bunker Hill in Boston
AUGUST 23, 1775:	King George III of England orders that the American rebels be put down by force
FALL 1775:	An American expeditionary force invades Canada
JANUARY 1776:	British warships bombard and burn Norfolk, Virginia; Thomas Paine's *Common Sense* is published
MARCH 1776:	The British evacuate Boston
JUNE 1776:	British warships bombard Charleston, South Carolina; the Americans retreat from Canada
JULY 4, 1776:	The Second Continental Congress approves the Declaration of Independence

Selected Bibliography

The Declaration of Independence is a living document that each generation interprets anew. The most authoritative and illuminating account of our time is Pauline Maier's *American Scripture: Making the Declaration of Independence* (New York: Alfred A. Knopf, 1997). I am indebted to that book and to Maier's informative introduction to the Bantam Classic edition of *The Declaration of Independence and The Constitution of the United States* (New York: Bantam Books, 1998). And I am grateful for the many insights in Carl Becker's classic work, *The Declaration of Independence: A Study in the History of Political Ideas* (New York: Vintage Books, 1958; originally published in 1922).

For my discussion of Thomas Paine's *Common Sense*, I turned to *The Thomas Paine Reader*, edited by Michael Foot and Isaac Kramnick (New York: Penguin Books, 1987).

Among the many fine narrative histories of the revolutionary period, I found particularly helpful Benson Bobrick's *Angel in the Whirlwind: The Triumph of the American Revolution* (New York: Simon & Schuster, 1997) and Thomas Fleming's *Liberty: The American Revolution* (New York: Viking, 1997). My account of the Boston Tea Party benefited from Wesley S. Griswold's detailed *The Night the Revolution Began: The Boston Tea Party, 1773* (Brattleboro, Vermont: The Stephen Greene Press, 1972). For my discussion of African-American soldiers in the Continental Army, I consulted Charles Johnson and Patricia Smith's *Africans in America: America's Journey through Slavery* (New York: Harcourt Brace & Company, 1998).

Esther Forbes's *Paul Revere and the World He Lived In* (Boston: Houghton Mifflin, 1942) is an absorbing portrait of Revere's life and times. David Hackett Fischer's scholarly *Paul Revere's Ride* (New York: Oxford University Press, 1994) offers fresh insights into that legendary event and the coming of the American Revolution. Other noteworthy biographical studies include Catherine Drinker Bowen's *John Adams and the American Revolution* (Boston: Little, Brown, 1950), Cass Canfield's *Samuel Adams's Revolution, 1765–1776* (New York: Harper & Row, 1976), Joseph J. Ellis's *American Sphinx: The Character of Thomas Jefferson* (New York: Alfred A. Knopf, 1997), Thomas Fleming's *The Man Who Dared the Lightning: A New Look at Benjamin Franklin* (New

York: William Morrow, 1971), Eric Foner's *Tom Paine and Revolutionary America* (New York: Oxford University Press, 1976), Willard Sterne Randall's *George Washington: A Life* (New York: Henry Holt, 1997), and Esmond Wright's *Franklin of Philadelphia* (Cambridge, Mass.: Belknap Press of Harvard University Press, 1986).

George F. Scheer and Hugh F. Rankin's *Rebels and Redcoats: The American Revolution Through the Eyes of Those Who Fought and Lived It* (New York: World Publishing Company, 1957) is a narrative account of the revolutionary era filled with the firsthand impressions of soldiers, statesmen, and civilians. Henry Steele Commager and Richard B. Morris's *The Spirit of 'Seventy-Six: The Story of the American Revolution as Told by Participants* (New York: HarperCollins, 1975) is a massive compilation of revolutionary-era documents, an essential resource for anyone researching this period.

Recommended books for young readers include Natalie S. Bober's *Abigail Adams: Witness to a Revolution* (New York: Atheneum, 1995), Barbara Brenner's *If You Were There in 1776* (New York: Simon & Schuster, 1994), Dennis Fradin's *Samuel Adams: The Father of American Independence* (New York: Clarion Books, 1998), James Cross Giblin's *The Amazing Life of Benjamin Franklin* (New York: Scholastic Press, 2000), Joy Hakim's *A History of US: From Colonies to Country* (Oxford University Press, 1993), Milton Meltzer's *The American Revolutionaries: A History in Their Own Words, 1750–1800* (New York: HarperCollins, 1987), and John B. Severance's *Thomas Jefferson: Architect of Democracy* (New York: Clarion Books, 1998). Jean Fritz is the author of a number of popular books about the revolutionary period, among them *Can't You Make Them Behave, King George?*, *And Then What Happened, Paul Revere?*, and *Will You Sign Here, John Hancock?* (all published in Paper Star by Putnam).

Illustration Credits

The prints and illustrations in this book are from the following sources and are used with permission:

Abby Aldrich Rockefeller Folk Art Center, Williamsburg, Virginia: page 11

American Antiquarian Society: pages 9, 70

Chrysler Museum of Art, Norfolk, Virginia. Gift of Edgar William and Bernice Chrysler Garbisch: page 10

Colonial Williamsburg Foundation: pages 24, 27

Delaware Art Museum. Museum Purchase, 1912: page 52

The Granger Collection, New York: pages 19, 40, 42, 47, 50, 64, 72

Courtesy of the Harvard Portrait Collection, President and Fellows of Harvard College. Bequest of Ward Nicholas Boylston, 1828, to Harvard College: page 21

Library of Congress: pages vi, 7, 8, 12, 13, 14, 16 (both), 17, 18, 20, 25, 29, 30, 36, 37, 39, 43, 45, 46, 48, 49, 53, 54, 55, 56, 58, 59 (bottom), 60, 61, 63, 65, 66, 69 (both), 74

Massachusetts Historical Society: page 59 (top)

Courtesy of the Museum of Fine Arts, Boston. Reproduced with permission. © 1999 Museum of Fine Arts, Boston: pages 28, 31, 34

The Pennsylvania Academy of Fine Arts, Philadelphia. Bequest of Mrs. Sara Harrison (The Joseph Harrison, Jr. Collection): page 6

Stock Montage: pages 3, 35

Yale University Art Gallery, Trumbull Collection: jacket, pages ii, 68

Index

Index

Index